MY TAKE

9

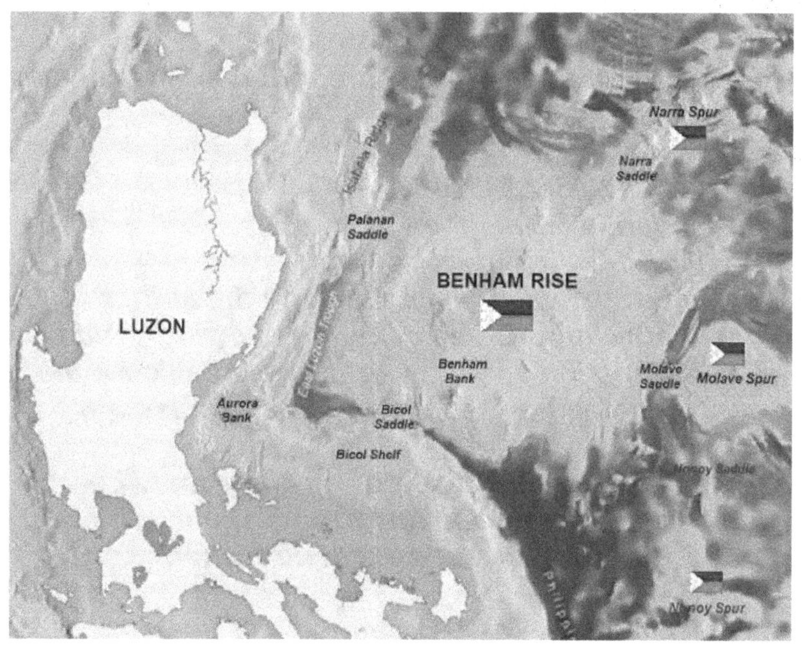

RAFAEL E. EVANGELISTA

AUGUST 2023

Published in USA in August 2023 by
TATAY JOBO ELIZES,
Self-Publisher, under the permission and
authorization of

RAFAEL E. EVANGELISTA
author and copyright owner.

KDP ISBN: 9798853362079
Independently Published

Contact: job_elizes@yahoo.com +
https://www.facebook.com/rafael.evangelista.5036459 +
http://tinyurl.com/mj76ccq (amazon site) +
www.tatayjoboelizes.webs.com +
https://www.facebook.com/groups/399368500835109

Cover image: Benham Rise, a Philippine territory,
per United Nations Resolution

....

Author

About the author:

Rafael E. Evangelista is a retired capital partner of Baker McKenzie, the largest international law firm in the world.

This is the resume' of Rafael E. Evangelista –

Lawyer, banker, diplomat.
Co-founder, Task Force Good Governance;
Board member, Bank of Commerce (former vice-chairman and executive committee member);

Various memberships in corporate boards including the Rizal Chapter and the Makati branch of the Philippine National Red Cross;
Board chairman of the NOVA Foundation for the Less Abled;

National Commander, Defenders of Bataan and Corregidor;

and Honorary Consul of the Republic of Lithuania to the the Philippines.
Retired Capital Partner, Baker & Mckenzie

(international law practice),
and Member, Board of Trustees, Ateneo de Manila
University.

Attended Ateneo de Manila University (A.B., LI.B.),
Georgetown University (Master of Laws), with an
honorary Ph.D. from St. Louis University. Recipient
of the Lithuanian Congressional Gold Medal of
Honor.

....

Dedication

Dedication I would like to dedicate this first, and hopefully not last, compendium of essays and poetry written by me to the following:

1. My parents, **Dr. Rafael E Evangelista** and **Encarnacion E. Evangelista**. My father was a real life war hero and a medical doctor who healed at no cost to his patients. In many ways, he was my life's inspiration of "service to others." My mom was the first real writer in the family. It was she who first encouraged me to write at an early age.

2) My sister, **Rhona E. Centeno**, the other real writer in the family with my mom. She won multiple award for her literary writings. She graduated with two Summa Cum Laude degrees, both completed in four years.

3) **Father Joseph O'Hare S.J.** was my freshman professor in English. He was a pillar of encouragement to my writing. He was the first person who insisted that I publish my works.

4) **Father Miguel Bernad S.J.** was the moderator of the Heights, the literary publication of the Ateneo. He caused the publication of some of my works to encourage me to share my writings with others.

I dedicate this book to these five persons who played such a singular role, each of them, in my literary life. Thank you.

....

Preface and Acknowledgment

Writing has been a passion of mine for almost as long as I can remember. I recall writing essays, short stories and poems as early as the age of 12 years.

Unfortunately, collecting and publishing whatever I had written never warranted the same attention I had given to writing them. Many, if not most of my articles and poems were lost over the years, with little recollection on my part of what, when, and where I wrote. Only a few were ever published.

Most of what I wrote had been scribbled on notebooks and left to fade on forgotten bookshelves. With the advent of computers and cellular phones, my writings were confined to the memory banks of these machines. As the machines turned obsolete, whatever writings were in them were simply confined to oblivion because I never transcribed what I had written.

Obviously, printing and publishing what I had written in the past did not occupy any position of priority in my mind's scheme of things.

I had been writing for many, many years simply for the joy of writing, and the joy of writing was for my self-fulfillment alone. I felt no need to share my thoughts, my dreams, my ambitions with anyone.

Or so I thought!

An old Jesuit professor of mine, Fr. Joseph O'Hare, S.J., who went on to become the President of Fordham University years later, was the first person to jiggle the notion that writing is only half the task of, well, writing! He told my parents at the end of my freshman year at the Ateneo de Manila University that their son was "intellectually selfish." He told them that I had refused to publish anything I had written, even in the school literary digests. The term he actually used to describe me was "intellectual bum."

Fr O'Hare complained to my parents that I had shown no interest in publishing, and hence in sharing, any of my writings. In so many words, he was telling my parents that while I had the talent to write, I was too selfish to share. Fr O'Hare's words did not sink in for many years.

A few years afterwards, another Jesuit professor, Fr. Miguel Bernad S.J., actually had some of my pieces published in the literary magazine of the Ateneo, The Heights, without my knowledge. As before, I had no interest in publishing what I wrote. And Fr. Bernad felt he had to take matters into his own hands.

Giving back was all this fuss was about. My two Jesuit professors and my parents were complicit in reminding me through the years that if someone had been given a gift, the gift was meant to be shared. Writing was only half of my life's mission of writing. Publishing and sharing with others completed the giving back required.

Although I have self published a number of Haiku poetry books over the past couple of years, this book "My Take 1" is the first comprehensive presentation of my writings - essays and poetry alike. For this effort, I have a new found friend, Jobo Elizes, from across the seas in the United States who encouraged me to publish this book, and beyond that, offered to publish the book himself.

I am grateful to my parents, Fathers O'Hare and Miguel Bernad S.J., and Jobo Elizes for all their encouragement that finally resulted in the publication of this book. I am likewise very grateful to have been afforded the opportunity of giving back and sharing with others, and hope my efforts are worth the reader's while.
Rafael E Evangelista 12 May 2023

....

Contents

....

1
Is The Philippines A Part Of China's Continental Shelf? China May Be Planning To Claim It Is! (Benham Rise)

I wrote this in April 2015. Am reposting to share:

Is The Philippines A Part Of China's Continental Shelf? China May Be Planning To Claim It Is!

The Unclos 200 mile exclusion zone is calculated from a country's continental shelf. We claim that China is building all these islands in the Spratlys and other areas within the West Philippine Sea far beyond the 200 mile exclusion zone of what the rest of the world considers is China's continental shelf, the shelf jutting from the mainland.

But what if China is not following the same calculations as the rest of the world? Remember China is claiming almost all of the China Sea, including what we call the West Philippine Sea, as part of the territory of China, independent of Unclos. In making this claim of ownership, China makes no reference either to Unclos or its continental shelf. Could it be that China's real intention in building and reclaiming islands in this area is so that it can later claim that its continental shelf starts with these islands, and the 200 mile exclusion zone should be calculated from them?

Using this formula, the Philippines could end up in a struggle with China on where China's continental shelf ends and where the Philippine continental shelf begins. The Philippines could very well lose all the seas along our western seaboard to a stronger and more powerful China. And China's claims may even go beyond our western coasts!

Indeed, extending this thesis, could China claim that the land mass of the Philippines, or a portion of it, particularly Luzon and the Benham Rise, are part of China's continental shelf? If China is claiming the entire "China Sea" as an "inland" sea that is part of the mainland, it does not take great leaps of logic to arrive at the possibility that China will also claim that its continental shelf starts at the boundaries of that "inland sea" comprised by the island chain it claims to own. This notion for now seems extremely far fetched. But then who would have imagined that just a few years ago China would claim all of the "China Sea" and start building islands within "spitting" distance of the Philippines.

I remember a meeting in 1977 I had in HongKong when I resided there before its return to Mainland China. My meeting was with an official from the Mainland. He told me then that China had territorial claims not only to the Philippine seas but also to its territory. Bob Romulo, the former Secretary of Foreign Affairs, also told me of a similar incident. Bob told me that during his father's time, China's Chou En Lai told his father, Carlos P Romulo, that the Philippines is part of China. I have never been able to personally confirm this statement attributed to Chou En Lai.

But what is happening today in our seas seems be an assertion and implementation by China of those claims. The Philippines could be surprised one day to find China claiming the resource rich Benham Rise in the Pacific Ocean off the Quezon and Aurora side and eastern seaboard of the Philippines as part of its continental shelf. Should all countries whose territories are bounded by the "China Sea" be put on notice that their territorial integrity may, even now, be at peril?

Rafael E Evangelista 29 April 2015

(Rafael Evangelista is a Retired Capital Partner of the International Law Firm of Baker & McKenzie)

....

2
To A Love Departed

I feel your presence
In the shower that falls
To water the blooms
That you left behind.
I touch you in the breeze
That gently blows across
The grass you walked.
I see your golden smile
In the rising sun above,
And hear the song
You used to sing at dusk
When angels came
To play with the moon
And the stars on high.
Heaven is now
Your eternal garden,
Which I see dancing
Up in the highest.
Yes, you are there!
I feel you,
I touch you,
I see you,

I hear you!
You are there!
And are here!
You are forever Mine!

(REE, 8 July 2023)

....

3
Marching Feet- Tribute to heroes on Memorial Day

I hear the beat of marching feet,
Feet gone beyond and over.
I hope to march along their way
Someday when life is over
To march beyond both night and day
To where is day all over.

(Rafael E Evangelista, 16 October 2020)

....

4

Where Have Bravery And Love Of Country Gone?

Have our "great and brave" current leaders issued any public, clear and categorical messages about this recent incidents of Chinese intrusion into our waters in the West Philippine Sea? And I am not speaking of reactions from the Philippine Coast Guard or the AFP. I speak of BBM and SD, the leadership of the Senate and the House. Have any of them filed complaints against China with the World Court or the UN?

I am one of those who are confused by the hemming and hawing of our l leaders. And this confusion is fast eroding the historical image of the Filipino who has fought for the cause of Philippine freedom and independence for centuries.

I personally weep for my father who fought the Japanese occupiers in WW II.

That is what the previous Administration of Dudirty did: offer to trade away our freedom and independence for the Philippines to become a province of China.

I weep for my grandfather and ancestors who fought the Spanish and American colonizers. Against all odds! They must all be weeping in their graves!

I weep for the Philippines!

(Raf Evangelista 8 July 2023)

....

5
Beyond The Right To Vote

It is about time the world, and the Philippines, moves away from the total emphasis on Governance by Leadership to a greater reliance on Governance by an informed and involved Citizenry. Democracy cannot mean simply the right of a citizen to elect the leader every four or six years, and in between do nothing and have no rights or responsiblilties of governance, except to hope for the best.

That is not Democracy. That is Feudalism that could lead to Populism, that could lead to despots and tyrants ..... that could lead to the death of Democracy.

Unbeknownst to many, that we already have provision for this in our Constitution and in law in the Philippines:

SOVEREIGNTY RESIDES IN THE PEOPLE AND ALL GOVERNMENTAL AUTHORITY EMANATES FROM THEM.

Our modern day tragedy in our Country is that Filipinos do not know or care that we have been provided by the Constitution and existing laws with the structure and the tools at People level, at Barangay level, to start a nationwide GOVERNANCE OF, FOR, AND BY THE PEOPLE!

Democracy does not, and cannot, simply mean the right to vote. We must govern at Barangay level through our Barangay Assemblies!

(REE, 9 November 2019)

....

6
THE STRONGER OR WEAKER SEX?

Is man, as most men are wont to claim, truly the "stronger sex?"

This seems to be the predominant and firm belief in the so called "battle of the sexes" that has been bandied around for generations, indeed for centuries. One only has to read recorded history, and one will appreciate that it is mostly male figures who dominate the model roles of national leadership and strength. So it seems logical to conclude that men are the stronger sex.

Wrong!

-Unless we recall the Biblical story of Adam and Eve, and man's first recorded sin. It was Eve after all who led Adam, at the coaxing of the serpent, to take that fateful bite of the apple. Eve was not a follower. She led and Adam followed.

-Unless we recall that the real heroes of the home are the wives. They do the child bearing and most of the child rearing in the family. They cook. They keep house. And all the other 12 to 24 hour tasks they have to attend to at home, including caring and spoiling the husbands who are "too tired" from 6 to 8 hour work shifts to lift a hand to help their wives at home.

What is amazing is how most women do not have to resort to force or threats to get their men folk to do their bidding. Like Eve, they use their considerable intelligence, and what God seems to have reserved exclusively for them, their feminine wiles and sultryness to in fact take the lead in most families and homes, while their men watch TV.

The explanation is simple (or complicated, depending on one's perspective).

Have you heard of the old adage: "The stronger sex is the weaker sex because of the weakness of the stonger sex for the weaker sex?"

Or in its other version:

"The weaker sex is the stronger sex because of the weakness of the stronger sex for the weaker sex?"

Some people actually go far to advance that this is the real reason why women, as a rule, outlive men. If accurate, this justifies the conclusion that women are in fact the stronger sex.

I first heard one or the other of the two versions of the old adage from my mother who, with an impish smile on her face, told my father about it. The response of my father was a puzzled "Huh?" He got caught like a fly in a trap by his own wife, my mother.

You guys go figure which version is more apt for this discussion. I think some smart and wiley woman started both versions to confuse her man. Once you decide on the correct version, let it be the guiding truth of your relationship with the fairer, and stronger sex!

The reality is that men have gotten so confused by this simple adage, they have lost years of their lives trying to figure it out. And that is why women live longer than men.

Actually, men lose out is either version of the adage. The net conclusion from both versions is that the women …. end up the winners in the shuffle.

Hahaha!

(REE, 15 April 2019)

....

7

I March With You In Spirit

I wrote this 3 years ago:
I March With You In Spirit

This 80 year old is with all who march for freedom, independence today, including the freedom of speech and of the press. I am one with you in spirit even if I can no longer keep in step with you.

God bless you all for loving our country where others do not; for defending our democracy even when others would trade it away; for defending the constitutionally proclaimed Sovereignty of the People even when others would falsely claim it as their own.

Freedom of speech, of the press and the right to peaceably protest is inherent in every person from the moment of birth. This is recognized by and in our Constitution. No law or regulation can be validly passed and enforced abridging these rights, peaceably exercised.

Under the Constitution, sovereignty resides in the People and all government authority emanates from them. You, the People, have endorsed that power to your servant leaders. Your servant leaders are at all times accountable and answerable to you, because you, the People, are Sovereign!

These are times when those elected servants have failed you, the people, the real Sovereign, multiple times! They must be held to account for what they have done, or failed to do.

God bless and protect us all!

(REE, 11 July 2020)

....

8
BAGUIO'S LOST LION'S HEAD

I raise an issue that may at first blush appear insignificant and irrelevant : The disappearance of the REAL LION'S HEAD ON KENNON ROAD ON THE WAY TO BAGUIO CITY.

But I believe that there is real significance and importance to that loss for all of us.

The issues are:

1) Was there another Lion's Head on Kennon Road on the way to Baguio City before the current Lion's Head that is now located there? And

2) Was the disappearance of the original Lion's Head located on Kennon Road due to man's callousness and self-centeredness, and an apparent lack of concern of man for nature and the environment?

The major entry point to Baguio City, the summer captial of the Philippines, is the historic Kennon Road built by the Americans during the US colonial period of the Philippines. Along the Kennon Road, THERE USED TO BE a unique, imposing and majestic natural rock formation of granite which locals and tourists alike marveled at.

Every summertime, when we were younger, my siblings and I would crane our necks as we drove up to Baguio for the summer holidays. We did so in anticipation of seeing this sculpture of nature which we and others called "The Lion's Head," because of the IMPRESSIONISTIC resemblance to the King of Beasts. This work of nature was imposing and regal.

Like any Natural Rock formation, a certain amount of imagination had to be utilized to pinpoint the classic features of the Lion in this imposing and massive natural piece of art. But it was precisely this partly abstract and partly impressionistic rendering that had made the ORIGINAL LION'S HEAD such an interesting and marvelous piece of art.

Needless to say, natural rock formations that seem to imitate life are exceedingly rare and need to be treasured. The Lion's Head of Baguio most closely replicated life of all the other natural rock formations in the Philippines that I was personally aware of. Being one of a kind, it was imperative that the Original Lion's Head be preserved at all costs.

Alas, sometime in the '70s (I believe), some small human minds, non-artistic and totally uneducated, spurred on by unbridled commercial infatuation, decided to interface with and deface this wonder of nature. This they did by re-sculpting, repainting the Original Lion's Face beyond recognition.

Try to imagine some misguided soul trying to paint over the walls of the Grand Canyon in the United States. Think of the protests and condemnations such act would bring down on the heads of the perpetrators. Think of the possible arrests and suits that that person would have to face as a consequence of his act of defacing nature.

Well, destruction and defilement of nature is what happened to the Original Lion's Head in Kennon. But with nary any arrests. The Lions Club of Baguio City, perhaps with the complicity of the City Government of Baguio, decided to "improve" on nature by creating a man made and uninspired sculpture of a new Lion's Head.

I have nothing against the Lion's Club or other socio-civic clubs. By and large, such clubs mean well, and do well by the communities they serve. But the current Lion's Head is one project of theirs that I strongly disagree with. They have debased a work of art of nature.

They have damaged the environment. It was an ill advised attempt on the part of the Lions Club of Baguio to gain advertising mileage for themselves. What they did to the Original Lions Head significantly unravels all the good work that the Lions have done for Baguio.

The result of their unmindful interference with nature is a grotesque and terrifyng head that only remotely resembles that of a lion. It looks more like a hand painted cross between a gorilla and some unknown monster, complete with giant fangs.

To add insult to injury, a giant sign of the Baguio's Lions Club has been attached to that monstrosity claiming that the sculpture was "constructed" by the Club, without clarifying what they had to first destroy to do so.

Today, younger generations gamely pose for pictures before this grotesque defilement of Nature's work, not realizing the historical and artistic loss that they incurred because of man's refusal to respect the environment. The young people have no idea of what Baguio has lost. And then I still have to hear any say that the current Lions Head on Kennon Road is anything but scary and terrifying.

In many ways, the LOST LIONS HEAD to my generation epitomizes the lost pine forests of Baguio, the denuded mountainsides, the massive informal settlements, logjams of traffic and pollution, and the dwindling visible indigenous culture of the City. Baguio could be a dying city.

It is a bitter lesson that we must pass on to the younger generations- that a failed environment will come back to haunt them. This is what the defilement of the ORIGINAL LIONS HEAD symbolizes for Baguio and all of us.

(Raf Evangelista, 18 April 2023)

....

9
Haiku Poetry
CONTEMPLATION

To be with you
Won'dring where you are,
Wan'dring to where you are,
To be where you are!
(REE, 19 August 2018)

Timeless
Seconds run with clocks
Which no longer tick away.
Time is timeless.

(REE, 20 August 2018)

Shared Destinies
You are, but I am.
Different, yet with shared dreams…
And shared destinies.
(REE, 21 August 2018)

Lost?
A child waves and smiles
While walking a lonely road.
He knows where he goes!
(REE, 22 August 2018)

Growing
Beyond eighty years,
I'll be brave enough to grow
And grow beyond then.
(REE, 23 August 2018)

Arms
The small girl hugged me.
Arms are for embracing,
I threw my gun away.
(REE, 24 August 2018)

On Fire
The rain is on fire.
Across incandescent skies,
Golden tears falling.
(REE, 25 August 2018)

Many Dreams
Where does the road lead?
Who can say as dark gathers?
Many dreams remain.
(REE, 26 August 2018)

Where?
And where was your heart

When you embraced and kissed me?
It had ceased to beat!
(REE, 27 August 2018)

Many Years Ago
I watched a small child
Form sand castles that
I built Many years ago.
(REE, 28 August 2018)

Contemplate
Ah! Now the moments
To sit still and contemplate
Beauty, love and you!
(REE, 29 August 2018)

United Force
See single raindrops
Race down the hillsides to form
The great sparkling sea!
(REE, 30 July 2018)

Flood Waters
Flood waters twist, turn.
Roaring tempests of the mind
Stir heaving waters.
(REE, 31 July 2018)

Is It Wrong To Be Right?
At day break, tears fall.
Why is it wrong to be right?
I don't understand!
(REE, 1 August 2018)

Reaching Out
My heart reaches out
To the star you travelled to
When you said, "Goodbye!"
(REE, 2 August 2018)

Colors Of The Wind
Gold and silver,
The colors of the wind
Blowing in the sun.
(REE, 3 August 2018)

Balance
The old man staggers
To keep his balance as his
Youth rushes past.
(REE, 4 August 2018)

Unsaid
The words "I love you"
Remained unsaid, even as
You walked away.
(REE, 5 August 2018)

I've Got You
Even with your back Turned,
I have got you covered
I embrace you, friend.
(REE, 6 August 2018)

Departure
Once the page is turned,
Will love depart once again,
As it did before?
(REE, 7 August 2018)

Stirrings
Memories fade, but
Why does the music still sing?
Echoes stir.
(REE, 9 August 2018)

Waiting
I will wait for you.
If the morning doesn't come,
You'll still find me here.

(REE, 10 August 2018)

Tribulus
Tribulus carpets,
The Kalahari sand dunes
With great mounds of gold.
(REE, 11 August 2018)

Dance Around The Rain
Drown out the darkness.
Whistle your song to the wind.
Dance around the rain.
(REE, 12 August 2018)

Deep Kiss
The hummingbirds kiss
Nectar filled blooms with deeply
Felt throated passion.
(REE, 13 August 2018)

Remenbering
Your tears in the shade,
Your laughter in the sunshine…
I remember you!
(REE, 14 August 2018)

Song To Remember
Cooing of the child,
A song in the heart chambers
Of the young mother.
(REE, 15 August 2018)

First Wheels
The old man gently
Caresses the old sedan,
His very first car.
(REE, 16 August 2018)

Stupor
The cold mountain wind

Washes away the stupor
Of last night's drinking.
(REE, 17 August 2018)

Throbbing
My head throbs wildly.
Is it from the many drinks,
Or from your kisses?
(REE, 18 August 2018)

Lapse of Time
Moments tick along
But memories race despite
The slow lapse of time.
(REE, 19 August 2018)

Thunder
The sky god claps his
Hands under the August skies,
Sending clouds weeping.
(REE, 20 August 2018)

Ninoy
Amidst yellow tears,
You laid your head down to rest
On the cold tarmac.
(REE, 21 August 2018)

Beyond The Ghetto
Through the shadows, hope
Stirs beyond the ghetto so
That light shines for all.
(REE, 22 August 20, 2013)

Your Song
Your love sings in me,
You touched my deepest being,
More than you can tell!
(REE, 23 August 2018)

Remembering
Slow days, hazy days.
In the warm embrace of love
Remembering you.
(REE, 24 August 2018)

Golden Promises
Morning breaks beyond
The dark tears of night, bringing
Golden promises.
(REE, 25 August 2018)

Plastic Forests
At water ends,
Mangled, tangled plastic ghosts
In drowning oceans.
(REE, 26 August 2018)

Why?
Why destroy our trees,
Our oceans, and our skies just
To feed our greed?
(REE, 27 August 2018)

Frantic Moment
Idle dark shadows
Scatter in frantic haste as
Street lights are switched on.
(REE, 28 August 2018)

Cupped Hands
The small child frolics
In the rain catching raindrops
With her two cupped hands.
(REE, 29 August 2018)

Goodbye
My tears flow slowly
As I bid my one brother

Goodbye at sunset.
(REE, 26 February 2014)

Embrace
The rain sings softly
As flowers bloom around you
Under dancing clouds.
(REE, 30 August 2018)

What Use, Words
Words shake, words break, words
Sometimes hate, but ahhh words soothe,
Inspire and even love.
(REE, 1 September 2018)

Winter Sun
The winter sun casts
Flickering flames on the crest
Of the freezing sea.
(REE, 2 September 2018)

Calling
My Beloved's voice
Sings among the westerlies,
Guiding me homewards.
(REE, 3 September 2018)

Eggshells
I cannot, will not
Walk on eggshells.
Destroy them Yourself, if you must.
(REE, 4 September 2018)

The First Star
At dusk, the small boy
Climbs the ladder in the yard
To touch the first star.
(REE, 5 September 2018)

Ethereal

Spirit Ethereal, fragile
Spirit fleeting by: butterfly,
Fly away with me.
(REE, 6 September 2018)

Crimson Gold
New stars tickle the
Old sun to draw one more burst
Of crimson gold.
(REE, 7 September 2018)

....

10
A Poem To An Eighty Year Old – Boogie Rodrigo

Now that you have reached a milestone - 80 years of age - permit me to share a poem I wrote for the occasion.

The poem is entitled:

THE MAN, A YOUTH

Endings are part of beginnings.
Sunsets are part of sunrises,
But beginnings never end.
Relish and live the later years,
and still love the taste of life.

The 80 year man, trudging
down the darkening walkway.
In the twilight, arms spread,
making like a bird flying

in the updrafts of the evening breeze….
There is so much still of the youth
In the 80 year old man.

But the grown man is not alone.
All stories eventually converge
like stones rolling into each other
beneath depths of a gliding river.
The man is blessed with a life
shared deeply with loved ones.
He is consoled in his autumn years.

His life can no more be separated
from lives of those who care,
than rain parted from clouds.
Like autumn leaves embraced
By the golden rays of the sunset,
Love, lives and years intersect,
and his life links time and lives.

There is a balance to it all:
Young life slows, a wise life grows.
Life and years are parts of a whole.
His life and years touch friends still. I
n time pieces of the puzzle will fit.

For now, the 80 year old man
soars with winds on wings of heaven,
the youth who yesterday was
learning how to fly!
Happy Birthday, Boogie!

Raffy

(Raf Evangelista, 18 July 2023)

………………………………..

11
Attorney-In-Fact As Part Of A Family

Attorney-In-Fact Within A Family

For starters, it is imperative that an Attorney in Fact never takes for granted the right to know of all of the family members. The holder of an SPA has the obligation and responsibility to give full, detailed and transparent reports to his principals, ie, his co-family members on a regular basis and/or as requested.

The rationale behind this obligation and responsibility is simply because the family members have a right to suggest, correct, agree or disagree on the terms of the Agreement, even if the SPA given to the Attorney in Fact does not specify restrictions or limitations.

The most basic right of the owners is to be informed of the net price they will be receiving AND to know and understand the process by which that net price was arrived at. To know and understand the process, the owners have the right to know what the gross price is, and if there is any differential between the gross and net prices, where that differential is going or will be used. This is the second basic right of the owners: the right to receive a full and adequate accounting of the utilization of funds/payments received. And this right of information must be given to the owners even before any Deed of Sale is executed.

The owners also have a right to know and to be assured that everthing done in relation to the contract will be done on a regular and legal basis, that all legal requirements for the validity and legality of the contract are complied with, AND that nothing has been done or will be done that is illegal or will invalidate the Agreement.

At the end of the day, an Attorney in Fact is still an agent of his principals, the owners. The latter are legally answerable for the acts of their agent.

(REE, 2021)

....

12
BADAC AND BARANGAYS

Btw, in the news today, "44,000 barangay anti drug abuse councils (Badac) nationwide have been activated in fighting criminality and drugs." (Inquirer, Tues, March 5, p A10). Also in the same article, "barangay chairs are mandated to submit a list of drug pushers/users and criminal elements in their respective jurisdictions to higher authorities. Inaction triggers heavy sanctions or removal from office. Loc Govt Undersecretary Martin Dino says he has been "firing one erring barangay chair daily." (ibid.)

I quite frankly meet this news with mixed emotions. I think the mobilization of the barangays to address or resolve national problems and concerns is in theory something that GBM has been espousing. But I worry that this program being implemented by the DILG could be placing the barangays totally under the control and direction of Dino, to the total exclusion of the barangay residents and their barangay assemblies.

Indeed, the Inquirer speaks only of the interaction in the program between the DILG and the barangay chairs.

Raf 2022

....

13
The Twelve Days of Christmas

There is one Christmas Carol that has always baffled me - The Twelve Days of Christmas.

What in the world do leaping lords, French hens, swimming swans, and especially the partridge who won't come out of the pear tree have to do with Christmas?

This week, I found out.

From 1558 until 1829, Roman Catholics in England were not permitted to practice their faith openly. Someone during that era wrote this carol as a catechism song for young Catholics.

It has two levels of meaning: the surface meaning plus a hidden meaning known only to members of their church. Each element in the carol has a code word for a religious reality which the children could remember.

• The partridge in a pear tree was Jesus Christ.

• Two turtle doves were the Old and New Testaments.

• Three French hens stood for faith, hope and love.

• The four calling birds were the four gospels of Matthew, Mark, Luke & John.

• The five golden rings recalled the Torah or Law, the first five books of the Old Testament.

• The six geese a-laying stood for the six days of creation.

• Seven swans a-swimming represented the sevenfold gifts of the Holy Spirit--Prophesy, Serving, Teaching, Exhortation, Contribution, Leadership, and Mercy.

• The eight maids a-milking were the eight beatitudes.

• Nine ladies dancing were the nine fruits of the Holy Spirit--Love, Joy, Peace, Patience, Kindness, Goodness, Faithfulness, Gentleness, and Self Control.

• The ten lords a-leaping were the Ten Commandments.

• The eleven pipers piping stood for the eleven faithful disciples.

• The twelve drummers drumming symbolized the twelve points of belief in the Apostles' Creed.

So this is your history for today. This knowledge was shared with me and I found it interesting and enlightening. Now I know how that strange song became a Christmas Carol.

Have a Meaningful Yuletide Season!

REE, 2022

....

14
An Insane MMDA Circular Dear Neighbors

I wrote this observation in 2021 at the height of the insane regulations that the authorities were promulgating to manage the pandemic-

An Insane MMDA Circular
Dear Neighbors:

What do you think of this and the MMDA circular on which it is based? I was told by my bank in Alabang, that I will not be allowed in, even at the bank! What about those above the age limit who have no one to assist them with their necessities?

Our neighbor and good friend, Ramon Fernandez is deathly ill. His wife is in her seventies. Their children are not always available to help their parents. Who will secure their needs?

The MMDA Circular and the implementing Ordinance of Muntinlupa make no exception. Does that mean I cannot go to the hospital for treatment? I am cancer victim and I do need treatment. Stretched to the ridiculous, it can mean that, since the circular's wording brooks of no exception, I myself cannot go outside for medical treatment.

But if in fact I am allowed to go for medical treatment, why can't I go out to buy food? Both the treatment and food are necessary!

I find the MMDA Circular and the Muntinlupa Ordinance ridiculous and probably unconstitutional.

REE, 2021

....

15
Dedicated to friends and relatives lost during this pandemic – Fly, Friends, Fly

FLY, FRIENDS, FLY

You hover over us in love,
Even as you had done ...
The sparkle of light above,
Just below the rising sun,
Is that you with angel wings
Amongst the clouds? You ...
Smiling, laughing, cheering
With the sparkle of dew?
There! On your radiant faces
The brillance of the sun
Reflecting Heaven's graces
On beloved, favored sons!
You have crossed over
From the dark to light.
Blue skies, no clouds to cover,
No darkness blocking sight.

No more dark fear tearing
At the heart's trembling skin.
Only gentle gazes looking,
Caring, loving from within.
You were the breath of spring,
From our friendship's start.
You taught us how to sing,
You quietly touched the heart.

You were the gentle laughter

That sang on despite the rain,
You were gold smiles of wonder
Amidst God's grace again.
Now, fly dear friends, from here
You are whole, you are free,
Free of pain, free of fear.
 God's love hearken unto thee!

Fly! FLY! Fly!

(Rafael E Evangelista, 6 May 2021)

....

16
Bonded

Family is not always related by blood. When you need someone, there sometimes is someone who is always there for you.

Together you two have a bond that draws him to see you through the most challenging situations, although you are not related by blood to each other.

Many times, a bond founded on the heart, soul and intellect can be more meaningful and lasting than a bond based on love alone.

That friend is family! Happy Birthday, Family!

Raffy 2023

....

17
A LETTER OF PRESIDENT EMILIO AGUINALDO

Whether you are an admirer of Aguinaldo or not, consider what he writes and its relevance to the claim of our political leadership it is useless to resist the encroachment of China into Philippine territory:

RESPONSE TO SR. BENITO LEGARDA WHO WAS URGING HIM TO SURRENDER TO THE SUPERIOR MIGHT OF AMERICA

"Personal.
"REPUBLICAN GOVERNMENT OF THE PHILIPPINE ISLANDS,
"OFFICE OF THE PRSESIDENT,
"Tarlac, September 14, 1899. ...

I must tell you that it is impossible for me to turn back from the enterprise which I have undertaken -that of defending our country, and especially as I have sworn that as long as life lasts I shall labor until I gain the acknowledgment of the independence of the Philippines... This, aside from the fact that the struggle for the independence of our country is just and based upon our perfect rights.

"We are not alarmed by the numerous arms nor the valor of our enemy. What is life to us if we are to be the slaves of the foreigner?... I repeat, we will not give up the struggle until we gain our longed-for independence: death is of but little moment to us if we are but able to ensure the happiness of the people and of future generations.

"We must no longer allow ourselves to be fascinated by the flattering promises of the enemy....

They have been using explosive bullets since the 9th of August last, and have bombarded defenseless forts, contrary to the precepts of international law. But it matters not that they use these elements of destructive warfare. Resistance and firmness of our resolution will be sufficient to wear them out. If this is not enough to induce our enemies to desist from their endeavor, we will go, if necessary, into the mountains, but never will we accept a treaty of peace dishonorable to the Philippine arms and disastrous to the future of the country, such as that which they seek to impose. "...

One should never repent of a just determination.

"Kind regards to your family, and to Messrs. Arellano, Pardo, Torres, and other friends.

"Command at will your most affectionate friend,

"E. AGUINALDO."

Repost

....

18
How Democracies Die

EDUCATION PROGRAM. Justice Tony Carpio said in his opening remarks of a media event that 1Sambayan is a coalition of democratic forces. He did not use the word opposition to define 1Sambayan. He preferred the phrase "democratic forces." He described the coalition as something engaged in the education program of our people. This is a major function of the coalition. Hence, it forms part of the voters' education to enable the people to understand the importance and significance of the 2022 presidential elections.

In their classic book "How Democracies Die," authors Steven Levitsky and Daniel Ziblatt we have to distinguish potential authoritarians so that they would not attain power and impose dictatorship to the misfortune of our people. They are easily discernible. They could even seen even from a distance. Levitsky and Ziblatt have given the following guide to know the potential authoritarians:

1. Rejection and weak commitment to democratic rules. Authoritarians like to cut corners. They have disdain to established democratic rules. "To remedy the ills of a democracy, we have to have more democracy," a noted political scientist said.

2. Denial of legitimacy of their political opponents. They condescend on their opponents, treating them with contempt and belittlement.

3. Encouragement of violence. They would not hesitate to use violence to attain their ends. They have armies, or armed groups to sustain violence.

4. Readiness to curtail civil liberties of rivals and critics. They are not afraid to EJKs.

Candidates who posses these qualities, should be rejected. We saw how the American people have rejected Donald Trump in 2020. We should not allow these candidates to take hold in our country. 2021

....

19
Highest Praise: ME WE - Ubuntu

"Yu, u nobuntu," the highest praise in African: you have the wonderful quality of "ubuntu." Ubuntu addresses a central tenet of African philosophy, the essence of what it is to be human - first, a person should use his strengths on behalf of others, and not take advantage of anyone. And second, a person should share his worth. In so doing one's humanity is recognized and inextricably bound with the others. The essence of ubuntu is "ME WE." The only way we can be human IS together. The only way we can be free IS together.

Raffy Evangelista, 4 September 2015)

Repost of anecdote about "Ubuntu":
An anthropologist played a game with some children of an African tribe.

He placed a basket full of fruit under a tree and told them: 'The first child to reach the tree will get the whole basket'

When he gave them the start signal, he was surprised that they simply walked together, holding hands, until they reached the tree and shared the fruit!

When he asked them why they did that, they answered: "Ubuntu" "How can one of us be happy while the rest are miserable?"

Ubuntu means: 'I am, because we are'.

Those young tribal kids understand the entire principle of life and the true source of happiness. The whole world needs to understand 'Ubuntu', that's what this awakening is all about.

CTTB

....

20

Racism Against Asian Americans, Including FilAms

The growing incidence of racism against Asian Americans is so distressing. But racism against Asians, specially Filipinos, is not a recent happening.

American racism against Filipinos dates back for over 120 years.

Remember when Filipinos were displayed in G strings at the New Orleans World Fair? Then there was the massacre of Filipino migrant workers in California (for dating white women), the reference to Filipinos as "monkeys" without tails; and the blanket claim by some white Americans that Filipinos who fought in WW II were all cowards. And what was the pretext given to justify US colonization of the Philippines? "To christianize and educate the savages in those islands." Ironically, these "savages" were largely Christianized and cultured by then. The list of racism incidents against Filipinos goes on and on.

To this day. Most Americans do not know or understand that, unlike other Asian countries, the Philippines was forcibly colonized in 1898 by the US. During that period, until 1946 when independence was finally granted, Filipinos were American nationals and, for those who travelled abroad, holders of US passports. No other Asian group fall into this category. The Philippines was the first, and officially the only colony of the United States. Filipinos are the only Asians who at one time in their history were American nationals.

Despite being forcibly colonized by the US, despite the fact that Filipinos fought the Philippine American War against American invaders only a few decades before WW II, and despite the fact that thousands of Filipinos lost their lives in their fight for freedom against the American colonizers, the Philippines threw in their lot to fight with and for America in WW II. The Philippines lost over a million of its young fighters and Filipinos civilians in WW II. Filipinos fought and/or sacrificed their lives, not only for the Philippines, but also for the US.

America still has to understand that the decision of the Philippines/US to stand together during WW II was less a decision of the United States to save the Philippines in the cause of Freedom and Democracy, as it was a decision of the Philippines to fight with the US. After all, Japan had promised the Philippines "independence," (which the Filipinos had long been fighting for) within the "Japanese Co-Prosperity Sphere" proposed by the Japanese. Filipinos could have easily sided with Japan in WW II against their "American oppressors" and gone with Japan who promised them immediate "freedom." If the Philippines had done so, there is arguably the possibility that America would have lost WW II. But that is another story.

In a limited sense, some recognition has been given by America to Filipino Veterans who fought in WW II. They were awarded in 2017 the highest civilian award that US Congress can give - the US Congressional Gold Medal, the first ever recipient of which was President George Washington himself. They were given that medal not just as Filipinos, but as American nationals as well. Incomplete recognition at best, but this USCGM in a way confirms a right of FilAms to reside in the US. They are after all, in a manner of speaking, "Gold Medal" FilAm descendants of their Filipino/American Veteran forebearers.

FilAms can point to the "trial by combat" that their Veteran forebearers went through in WW II. They can assert that their forebearers fought in that War not simply as Filipinos but as American nationals, not simply for the Philippines, but for America. As an Asian American veteran (not a FilAm) declared as he showed his scars of war on TV: "Is this patriot(ic) enough?"

I hasten to point out another fact. Thousands of Filipinos are even now in the forefront of another war for the US. Thousands of Filipino nurses and doctors are quietly fighting the Pandemic War today as medical frontliners. In California alone, there are at last count over 30,000 nurses on the Pandemic frontlines. If all FilAm medical frontliners in the US came home to the Philippines today because of the threat of racism, the health systems of some States of the Union, and maybe the US itself, could collapse and many more Americans would perish.

Historically too, Filipino settlements existed in the America long before the Pilgrims came. The arrival of the Pilgrims is, of course, the corner stone of White America's claim to the US. But the ties between Filipinos and America started long before the Pilgrims arrived. If Filipinos arrived in America before the Pilgrims, America has no basis for demanding that FilAms return to where they came from.

It is interesting but few people know that there may be linguistic and cultural ties between Filipinos and Native Americans. Take the similarities between Tagalog/other Philippine dialects and certain Native American languages. In the North Dakota Sioux language, the word for mother is "Ina", as it is in Tagalog. Do these language similarities give credence to the claim that migrations from our part of the world are, by virtue of sea and overland travel, related to Native Americans? Maybe so. Maybe our ancestors landed in America long, long before the Pilgrims did. Maybe they were there when Native Americans came to be.

I would like to add one other personal observation on "Race."

Quite frankly, I do not agree that people should be typed by the color of their skin. To begin with, there is no such thing as a "White" person. Put a white sheet of paper beside any "White" man. He will most certainly not be white. The so called "White" man is pink and all the shades from there to flushed red. So when some, and there are many, talk about people of color" to refer to the brown, black and yellow populations, the little bell of racism in my brain starts ringing.

Wittingly or unwittingly, the phrases "I am White" and you are a "Person of Color" is racism itself at its most insidious. It translates to "I am White! I am special and unique! All other races are colored and belong to the "hoipoloi." "People of Color" has become to some "White" people a pejorative to discriminate against non-whites. But these "White" bigots fail to realize and understand that they too are people of color. They too are non-whites!

Looking at legislation passed in the early years of America, it is clear that racism through legislation was a basic tenet that States like Virginia and Maryland implemented to create a privileged class of citizens that came to be what is now known as the "White Race." This legislation not only condoned and permitted slavery of "Black and Colored People", but enshrined the so called superiority of the "White Race." Under threat of severe penalties, people from the "Colored Races" could not marry or have sex with the "Whites." "Colored" persons could not vote run for public office or own property. As late as 1937, even Native Americans were not allowed to vote ... on the ground that they were not citizens!

In the 1950's, "Colored" people had to give up their seats to "White" people on crowded buses. Only "Whites" could sit in the front sections of those buses. I share an anecdote about a grandfather of mine, Col. Jose N Evangelista. Col Evangelista was the first Filipino Commandant and Superintendent of the Philippine Constabulary Academy (later the Philippine Military Academy) years before WW II and before Rosa Banks.This was during the period when the Philippines was still a colony of the US.

Col Evangelista was sent on a military mission to the US. He was riding public transportation in the full uniform of an officer in the US Army in Washington DC when he was told to move to the rear of the bus. His response was: "If I am entitled to use this uniform, I am entitled to sit in the front of this bus," and stayed where he was. But my grandfather was a rare exception. Few "Colored" persons were granted Officer rank in the US Army during his time.

It is unfortunate that today many "People of Color" have swallowed the lie, hook, line and sinker, that race is a determining factor of one's status in American society. It isn't, and certainly shouldn't be. Love, not race, is the determining factor in any family, in any community, and in any society. And love has no color.

In a spillover of the "war of colors," it is unfortunate that the war has taken a grotesque turn for the worse. Where the war before was principally between the "white" race and "people of color," the trend of late has been racist attacks by the "blacks" against Asian Americans or the yellow and brown races. The so called "people of color" are turning against one another.

Racism must stop in the United States. Because if it continues, "United" will be "Divided." And a "Divided States" will not survive!

The story of the relations between the US and the Philippines is a long, and sometimes a rocky, one. There is so much more to that story that can be written about here. But that story is one that most Fil Ams should learn about if they wish to claim their rightful place in American Society!

(Raffy Evangelista, 12 April 2021)

(Rafael E Evangelista is a retired Capital Partner of the International Law Firm of Baker & McKenzie, An immediate past National Commander of the Defenders of Bataan & Corregidor)

....

21
There Is Room

There is room in the sky

For more than just one star.
There is more than one tree
To be seen from afar.

We should not stand alone
In the heavens or on earth.
Rather, we stand together
From the moment of birth.

We are children of heaven
If we stay united in love,
With blessings that God
Has sent from above.

Look at the blossoms
That spring on dry land.
United they form rainbows
Of colors on sand.

Listen to the songs
Of birds from the trees,
The music they create
Along with the breeze.

Those silver dew drops
That sparkle like stars
In the early morning sun
Can be seen from afar.

Look to the sunset
Even as we pray,
One prism of colors
At the end of the day,

There is room in the sky
For more than just one star.
Let us all reflect His Love
From near and afar.

(Raf Evangelista, 17 April 2023)。

....

22
Love Laid Bare: An Easter Sunday Offering

This Easter, There is nothing better:

Than to be a light in the darkness,
Be the smile through the sadness.
There can be more happiness
If one is willing to share.

Though storms of bleakness,
You can bring back the loveliness,
If you will only give brightness
To those in your life, and care.

Joy is shared through thoughtfulness,
Love is given amidst loneliness,
To those stranded in aloneness,
Whose sadness is laid bare.

Amidst shadows of starkness,
Be the one who truly dares.
Plant the seed of Godliness,
Be one who sincerely cares!

Do try your best to love
As He did from above.
Sharing is the only way
We can ever truly say:

Thank You Lord For Easter Sunday!

(Raf Evangelista, 9 April 2023)

....

23
The Legend of Christmas

Tree Pious legend recounts that when the shepherds went to adore the Divine Infant, they decided to take Him fruits and flowers from the area. After this harvest, the plants congratulated themselves on being able to offer something to their newly-born Creator: one had given its dates; another its nuts, and so on.

From the fir tree, however, the shepherds had taken nothing because its needle-like leaves and sharp cones were not presentable gifts.

The fir tree recognized its unworthiness, and not feeling worthy to participate in the conversation, prayed in silence: 'My newly-born God, what can I offer You? I offer you my poor and unworthy existence. This I gladly give You in gratitude for having created me in Your wisdom and goodness.'

God was pleased with the humility of the fir tree, and, as a reward, ordered a multitude of little stars to come down from heaven to adorn it. The stars were of many colors: gold, silver, red, blue, all the colors of the rainbow. When a group of shepherds passed by, they not only took the fruits of the other plants, but they also took the whole fir tree, as such a marvel had never before been seen. Thus the fir tree ended up decorating the grotto of Bethlehem, being placed close to the Child Jesus, Our Lady, and Saint Joseph!

This is the legend of the Christmas tree.

CTTO

....

24
HAIKU MUSINGS (A LOT)

Within Without
Within, the joys of
Life and love and spring ... without,
The chills of winter.
(REE, 12 September 2020)

The Longest Moments
The second before
And second after ... moments
When darkness stood still.
(REE, 20 February 2021)

Beginnings And Endings
Not just beginnings.
Endings too are beautiful ...
Stars in the darkness.
(REE, 22 September 2020)

Reflections
Reflections of love
Between azure sea and sky,
Painting shifting dreams.
(REE, 11 October 2020)

Empty
Neon lights flashing
On wet, lonely pavements,
Reflect cold stillness.

(REE, 5 December 2020)

Ethereal
In the shimmering light,
I reached out to touch her face,
But she was not there.
(REE, 1 September 2020)

Flower
The lonely flower,
Discarded in the trash bin,
Bows its head and weeps.
(REE, 2 September 2020)

Two Stars
Two lights dance high up
In the night sky - a firefly
Waltzing with a star.
(REE, 6 March 2021)

The Dance
The old man dances
Around the floor to music
His wife used to love.
(REE, 6 March 2021)

Stranger
I do not know you.
So why is it that I feel
We loved once before?
(REE, 4 March 2021)

Meaning
If words are not said.
Every action undefined
Can mean for nothing.
(REE, 3 July 2022)

Too Late
Me, falling in love?

I never did (and what for?) …
Then you looked at me!
(REE, 3 July 2022)

In Love
I cannot help it.
Everytime I see you smile,
I know I love you!
(REE, 3 July 2022)

Smile
To smile takes seconds.
If you do not have the time,
Why should I then care?
(REE, 3 July 2022)

As Night Comes
Even as night comes,
I will be searching for you
Now that you are gone!
(REE, 3 July 2022)

My Hands
Look! My gnarled fingers.
Through the winter of my days
My hands planted life.
(REE, 1 September 2022)

White Fire
Once the line is crossed
Where white fire both burns and soothes,
There is no return.
(REE, 29 January 2020)

Love's Meaning
Building means giving,
But love simply comes to naught
Without forgiving.
(REE, 4 February 2020)

Once, Valentine
A kaleidoscope
Of many moments now flown
With Valentine gone.
(REE, 14 March 2020)

A Promise
I deny tonight
To be able to promise
Light for tomorrow.
(REE, 25 March 2020)

Friends
Hand in hand through years,
Sun soaked in the warmth of years,
Amidst wrinkled smiles.
(REE, 19 March 2019)

Cleansing Rain
The old horse plods in
The swirling mud, then canters
To the cleansing rain.
(REE, 20 March 2019)

Letting Go
I can let go of
Power and wealth, but not of
The love now distant.
(REE, 22 April 2019)

The Road
Don't pass up today,
Tomorrow may never come,
Since yesterday stayed.
(REE, 28 June 2019)

Listen to the Dark
Nothing to something...
Listen to the darkness and
Hear the light singing.

(REE, 15 October 2019)

Heaven's Fire

Fire from the heavens,
Deep rumblings before the storm,
The anvil of God.
(REE, 30 November 2019)

Soaring

I do not pander
To those who would push and shove.
Soaring, should I care?
(REE, 11 December 2019)

Kiss

Kiss dew drops falling
Over scorched, burning mountains.
Trees, what remain, weep.
(REE, 25 December 2019)

Trash

Trash in parks and roads,
Trash amongst those who would lead,
Trash in minds and hearts.
(REE, 27 December 2019)

Memories

I will write the hurts
On drifting sands, and etch my
Love on solid rock.
(REE, 4 January 2020)

Burning

The earth is burning.
Is it God's wrath or our own
Stupidity? Maybe both?
(REE, 5 January 2020)

Embers

In the despair of

Darkest winter burns softy
The embers of spring.
(REE, 6 January 2020)

Colored Glasses
Through the prism of
Colored glasses: softly Fall.
Then, Winter sharply.
(REE, 6 January 2020)

Home
Going home is just
Beyond the bridge of darkness
To light all over.
(REE, 7 January 2020)

Indifferent
I, indifferent?
Should I care, if you do not
Make a difference?
(REE, 8 January 2020)

War Rumblings
Flashes in the dark.
Drums of war rumble, but rains
Drench the roaring fires.
(REE, 11 January 2020)

Scorched
The tear slowly falls,
The last of many that fell.
The scorched heart rages.
(REE, 12 January 2020)

White Fire
Once the line is crossed
Where white fire both burns and soothes,
There is no return.
(REE, 29 January 2020)

Love of Self
Why must it be so?
There's a lot of self in you,
Taking, not giving.
(REE, 3 February 2020)

Love's Meaning
Building means giving,
But love simply comes to naught
Without forgiving.
(REE, 4 February 2020)

Unseen Piper
We all march to the
Tune of the unseen piper's
Haunting melody.
(REE, 5 February 2020)

Sister
I reach out my hand
To one I loved all these years,
Born from the same womb.
(REE, 5 February 2020)

Go Low, Why?
Why must we go low?
We can't go high anymore,
Because others won't?
(REE, 7 February 2020)

We Are More
They win by making
You feel that you are alone ...
There are more of us.
(REE, 9 February 2020)

My World
There is joy that's found
In simplicity of life,
The world I hope for.

(REE, 15 February 2020)

Populism
Not allowed to speak,
Not allowed to criticize,
The freedom bell tolls.
(REE, 29 February 2020)

Once, Valentine
A kaleidoscope
Of many moments now gone,
A portrait of love.
(REE, 14 March 2020)

Political Winds
Shifting of the winds,
Where will they carry me to,
Peace or turbulence?
(REE, 22 March 2020)

Distant Light
A faint light flickers,
A star or distant firefly.
In the dark, who knows?
(REE, 25 March 2020)

Whimper
In the darkness,
I Raised my hand to stroke my dog.
Faintly, a whimper.
(REE, 27 March 2020)

Taho
The vendor searches
Forlornly for the children
Who used buy taho.
(REE, 30 March 2020)

Hungry
Hunger stalks the land

From dark sea to fearful sea,
Waves from dark waters.
(REE, 1 April 2020)

On My Own
I bow my head as
I hear the clap of thunder.
I am on my own.
(REE, 10 April 2020)

Broken Pieces
I held out my hand.
You refused to walk with me...
Broken pieces fell.
(REE, 21 April 2020)

Fly With Me
Why do you have doubts?
Before the sun disappears,
Fly away with me.
(REE, 29 April 2020)

Silence
The laughter shattered,
A tear ripples on the pond,
Then awkward silence.
(REE, 12 May 2020)

Goodbyes
Why are there goodbyes?
Do things really have to end?
Go then. Say nothing.
(REE, 25 May 2020)

Life and Death
Defeat death in life.
Do not be pushed by darkness,
Till death takes you home.
(REE, 1 June 2020)

Heartbroken
I am heartbroken.
My soul may not remember
You, when I am gone.
(REE 30 June 2020)

Rusting
The junkyard filled with
Bones of old forgotten toys,
Rusting in the wind.
(REE, 10 July 2020)

Searching
Nothing is stirring,
But for a heart beat throbbing,
Searching for a love.
(REE, 21 August 2020)

One
Sunrise once again.
Beyond dark skies and thunder,
People will be one.
(REE, 21 July 2020)

Departure
Standing on the porch,
Watching you walk away, it
Seems like yesterday.
(REE, 25 July 2020)

Morning Wait
The morning will come
From where I shall keep waiting.
For now the night grows.
(REE, 1 August 2020)

Trapped Air
The mask clouds my breathe,
So that I can hardly breath
The air trapped outside.

(REE, 30 August 2020)

Long Way
On the lonely road,
Too far to travel back.
A long way ahead.
(REE, 22 September 2020)

Restive
The rumbling heavens
Stir up restive, restless clouds
With claps of thunder.
(REE, 25 September 2020)

Deaf Ear
You're so far away…
Can you even hear my voice?
You turned a deaf ear!
(REE, 5 October 2020)

Shadow Paint
Shadows race across
The grasslands, chasing after
Clouds that paint the sky.
(REE, 1 October 2020)

Night Embrace
I embrace the night
To be able to ensure
Light for tomorrow.
(REE, 21 October 2020)

Seeing The Light
It is in the dark That
I can see the sunlight
I close my eyes now.
(REE, 29 October 2020)

Endings?
Why are there endings?

Are evers not forevers?
Every moment lost?
(REE, 13 November 2020)

Lost Smile
I was crestfallen
I'd never see you again,
Smiling through the rain.
(REE, 19 November 2020)

Broken Pieces
Broken pieces of
Today dumped in the dust bins
Of forgotten days.
(REE, 22 November 2020)

Shut Door
It is storming outside,
But I do not really care.
I have shut the door.
(REE, 1 December 2020)

I Can't Breathe
Mama, I can't breathe!
The morning is turning dark.
Now I cannot see.
(REE, 1 June 2020)

Tears
I am drained of smiles...
Lost behind the drapes, the sun!
Please bless me with tears.
(REE, 4 June 2020)

Once More
Just before daylight,
Let me embrace you once more,
Before you turn to go.
(REE, 22 June 2020)

Take A Knee
We are connected,
All of our minds, hearts and souls.
Let us take a knee.
(REE, 1 July 2020)

Heart Light
I will walk with you
No matter the churning skies.
Your heart lights the way.
(REE, 7 July 2020)

Everybody smiles,
Everybody cries,
sometimes,
In rain and sunshine.
(REE, 15 July 2020)

Please Stay
Don't just turn away,
I have been waiting so long.
I ask you to stay.
(REE, 30 June 2020)

Time
To Let Go There's a void in me.
It's been fifteen years ago.
It's time to let go.
(REE, June 28, 2020)

Rainbows on the Desert Floor
Carpets of flowers
On the arid desert floor,
Rainbows without rain!
(REE, 27 August 2020) ∘

....

25
The Great I Am

I will speak the secret
Language of the trees,
And hum along with
The cooling breeze.
I will paint brilliant colors
Of the sunset in the west,
And shimmering morning's
Sunrise to the east.
I will scan stars shining,
Twinkling, twirling, dancing
In the heavens above.
I am, I shall be
Forever grateful,
Forever thankful
For the Great I Am,
And all His love
He gives to me.

(REE, 15 July 2023)

....

26

Please Return My Yesterday

There will be no goodbyes
If you return my yesterday.
There was nothing but
Sunshine that colored our path,

but sad to say
It did not end that way.
When you turned away
Without any goodbye,
All I heard was a sigh,
And I didn't know why.
Is it possible to return
To that solitary day
So love can still burn?
Return my yesterday.
Please do not walk away.
I will always love you:
Tomorrow, today, yesterday!
I love you still.
I always will.

(REE, 15 July 2023)

....

27

Repost: The Philippines was a takeover target of America even before China expressed any interest in our country. This is the response to those designs of the Philippine Leader at the time, Emilio Aguinaldo.-

A LETTER OF PRESIDENT EMILIO AGUINALDO-

Whether you are an admirer of Aguinaldo or not, consider what he writes and its relevance to the claim of our political leadership it is useless to resist the encroachment of China into Philippine territory:

RESPONSE TO SR.BENITO LEGARDA WHO WAS URGING HIM TO SURRENDER TO THE SUPERIOR MIGHT OF AMERICA

"Personal. "REPUBLICAN GOVERNMENT OF THE PHILIPPINE ISLANDS,

"OFFICE OF THE PRSESIDENT, "Tarlac, September 14, 1899. ...

I must tell you that it is impossible for me to turn back from the enterprise which I have undertaken -that of defending our country, and especially as I have sworn that as long as life lasts I shall labor until I gain the acknowledgment of the independence of the Philippines... This, aside from the fact that the struggle for the independence of our country is just and based upon our perfect rights.

"We are not alarmed by the numerous arms nor the valor of our enemy. What is life to us if we are to be the slaves of the foreigner?... I repeat, we will not give up the struggle until we gain our longed-for independence: death is of but little moment to us if we are but able to ensure the happiness of the people and of future generations.

"We must no longer allow ourselves to be fascinated by the flattering promises of the enemy.... They have been using explosive bullets since the 9th of August last, and have bombarded defenseless forts, contrary to the precepts of international law. But it matters not that they use these elements of destructive warfare. Resistance and firmness of our resolution will be sufficient to wear them out. If this is not enough to induce our enemies to desist from their endeavor, we will go, if necessary, into the mountains, but never will we accept a treaty of peace dishonorable to the Philippine arms and disastrous to the future of the country, such as that which they seek to impose.

"...One should never repent of a just determination.

"Kind regards to your family, and to Messrs. Arellano, Pardo, Torres, and other friends.

"Command at will your most affectionate friend,

"E. AGUINALDO."

Aguinaldo's reaction is a far cry from that of Rodrigo Duterte to China's designs over the Philippines. CTTO

....

28
Fr James B Reuter's Prayer On The Occasion Of The National Elections

Lord God: Look down upon us this day, this hour, regardless of what has gone before or what will come after. Give us the grace to consecrate ourselves and our Country entirely to you, all the actions of our bodies and souls.

In the midst of the worry and confusion wrought by these uncertain days of the pandemic, poverty, corruption, foreign transgressions, and political concerns, may all the thoughts that come to us be true; may all the things to which our hearts go out be beautiful with the Beauty of God; and free of fear and despair, and in complete surrender to Your Will, may all the things we want be good.

We pray that Your Healing Grace will turn darkness to light. And through this crisis, give Your people the grace to elect and appoint only Your anointed leaders to our Country's leadership. Grant our People the light to know Your Will, the grace to love It, the courage and strength to fulfill It, we ask You this through Jesus Christ, Your Son. Amen.

(Based on a prayer of Fr. James B Reuter S.J., with revisions by REE)

....

29
Pushing Back

Australia pushes back against China's campaign to infiltrate and influence: China's attempts in Australia are the same as their attempts in the Philippines, but the Philippines is not pushing back:

And it isn't just Australia that is pushing back against Chiina in our region. Taiwan and Vietnam have been pushing back for decades now. Indonesia and Malaysia are pushing back. Pakistan is starting to push back. South Korea has never allowed itself to be pushed around by China. Even North Korea, although politically aligned with China, is no puppet of China.

At the rate developments are happening, it may only be the Philippines that refuses to push back and resist China's overt and covert acts of aggression, all because we "cannot win the war against a bigger and stronger China."

The irony is the Philippines has one of the longest histories of fighting foreign aggression - Spain, America, Japan, and yes, even Limahong - in SouthEast Asia!

(REE, 2018)

....

30
The Sun God

The chatter
of the birds
fall silent with
the growing stillness
of the symphony
of deepening night.

The busy white
clouds that danced
to the blaze of
morning, retreat
silently at evening
to the home of

the golden sun,
now dressed with
in the colours of
his cloak:
an abstraction
of rainbow strokes.

And as evening comes,
the sun god,
knowing that
he soon must go,
tears up his robe
of prismatic colours,
and spreads it across
the western clouds
in benediction,
a fond farewell
and a promise
of his return
on the morrow.

His colours flame
and blaze, reflections
on the sea, whose
rouge - lipped waves
lap gently,
heaving ruby swells,
slowly, kaleidoscopically,
rocking the night
to a tantalizing deep
and profound sleep.

I slowly turn away from
the framed abstraction
in my window
of fading colors
of purple, blue,
orange and crimson.

*Reassured by
his promise that
he will return
in the morrow in a blaze
of gold and silver,*

*I slide into the gentle
embrace of the night,
the caressing breeze,
and the soft rustle of
the curtains, and
fall into a peaceful
slumber.*

(Raf Evangelista,
13 March 2023)

....

31
Gen. Edilberto Evangelista

I did not write this, but I thought it should see the light of print in my book, because Edilberto was an ancestor of mine. With due credits to the writer:

Gen Edilberto Evangelista

Early life and career Edit He was born in Sta. Cruz, Manila, on February 24, 1862. Evangelista finished his Bachelor of Arts at the Colegio de San Juan de Letran in 1878.[1] He was awarded a medal of excellence in Mathematics. Poor health made him to drop his idea of studying medicine. After this, he became a teacher, a cattle dealer, a tobacco merchant between

Cebu and Manila, and later a contractor of public works. He soon went to Madrid in 1890. It was during this time that he befriended many Filipino patriots, including José Rizal, who advised him to study engineering in Belgium.[1]

He therefore enrolled at the University of Ghent, one of the world's top engineering schools, and finished civil engineering and architecture with highest honors. He then received profitable offers of employment from several institutions in Europe but he declined because of his zeal to serve his country.

He returned to the Philippines in September 1896, shortly after the start of the Philippine Revolution. He was arrested and imprisoned, since the Spanish authorities suspected many people of the revolution and he had in his possession Jose Rizal's Noli Me Tangere and El Filibusterismo, but he escaped.

He joined General Emilio Aguinaldo's command on October 22, 1896.At the Imus Assembly on December 31, 1896, Evangelista had submitted his draft of a constitution as requested by both Magdalo and Magdiwang factions of the KKK. He was elected Lieutenant General in the said meeting, now in the ranks of Artemio Ricarte.

Aguinaldo later utilized General Evangelista's engineering skills. He planned and built forts and barricades in Bacoor, Binakayan, Cavite Viejo, Munting-ilog, Silang, Dasmariñas, Imus, Salitran, Lumang-bayan, and Noveleta, to serve as protection against Spanish forces.[3] One Spanish general commented that the fortifications were the "fortifications of the future."[1]

Aguinaldo himself publicly recommended Evangelista to head the revolutionary government that would be established in lieu of the Katipunan, for he was "the most educated" in the organization. Aguinaldo also said that Evangelista could "command the respect of the Spaniards".

He was part of the Magdalo government, serving as assistant overall captain general to Aguinaldo.

Though in the actual sense, he was neutral in the Magdalo-Magdiwang feud.

Evangelista was calm but fatalistic, a characteristic often interpreted as bravery. He was drawing trenches on the ground with a stick while the enemy fired cannons at their forces. One time, a shell dropped very near him yet he did not flinch nor run, instead he brushed the dust off his coat and continued to draw.

His life soon ended, as well as hopes for him by fellowmen, when he died, along with Captain Mariano San Gabriel and Captain Mariano Ramírez, on February 17, 1897 during the Battle of Zapote Bridge. His post was succeeded by his protégé, Miguel Malvar.[Parent organization Katipunan

It was named after Mary Magdalene, patroness of Kawit, Cavite. It was officially led by Baldomero Aguinaldo, but his cousin Emilio Aguinaldo (whose own Katipunan codename was "Magdalo") was its most famous leader.[1]:22

The Magdalo had a rivalry with the other Katipunan chapter in Cavite, the Magdiwang (both factions are terminologies for feasts: "dalo" in Tagalog means to attend, diwang means to celebrate). When the Manila-based Katipunan leader Andres Bonifacio went to Cavite to mediate between them, the Magdalo argued for the replacement of the Katipunan by a revolutionary government.[1]:90

The Magdiwang initially backed Bonifacio's stance that the Katipunan already served as their government, but at the Tejeros Convention, both factions were combined into one government body under Emilio Aguinaldo who was elected as the president.

Some of the civil and military officials of the First Philippine Republic came from this group.

Magdalo Leaders Edit
- • Baldomero Aguinaldo - President
- Edilberto Evangelista - Vice President
- Candido Tirona - Secretary of War
- Felix Cuenca - Secretary of Interior

- Glicerio Topacio - Secretary of Public Works
- Cayetano Topacio - Secretary of Finance
- Emilio Aguinaldo - Flag Officer

CTTO

....

32
The Final Smile

He said, "Don't call the doctor,
I want to fall asleep peacefully,
With your hand in mine."
They talked about the past,
How they met, their first kiss.
They didn't cry, they smiled.
They didn't regret anything,
They were grateful.
Then she repeated softly,
'I will love you forever!'
He returned her words,
Gave her a soft kiss
On her outstretched hand.
He closed his eyes with a smile,
and fell asleep peacefully
with his hand in hers, then left.
But the smile remained.

Rafael E Evangelista 5 September 2021

....

33
Security Risks

Why Mainland Chinese Nationals and Mainland Chinese Corporations could be security risks to the Philippines:

There is, of course, today the inflow into the Philippines of thousands of mainland Chinese nationals under the guise of investors, workers, gamblers, tourists, etc who have floooded our shores since Duterte took over the Philippine Government in 2016, potential spies all.

Why "potential?" And why "all?"

Of course, there have been denials by Chinese nationals and corporations that they are mainland Chinese spies. Huawei, a Chinese corporation from the mainland, has insisted that it does not, and will not spy for China even if compelled to do so.

But mainland China's 2017 National Intelligence Law states that "any (Chinese) organization or citizen shall support, assist and cooperate with the State intelligence work in accordance with the law." And China's 2014 Counter-Espionage law states that "when the State security organ investigates and understands the situation of espionage and collects relevant evidence, the relevant organizations and individuals shall provide it truthfully and may not refuse."

Given these provisions of mainland Chinese law, "there is no way Huawei (or any Chinese corporation or national for that matter) can resist any order of the People's Republic of China Government or of the Chinese Communist Party to do its bidding in any context, commercial or otherwise. This was the conclusion of Jerome Cohen, a New York University Law professor and Council on Foreign Relations fellow, as quoted in a CNBC report. He stated that "Huawei (or any mainland Chinese corporation or national would have to turn over all requested data and perform whatever other surveillance activities are required."

This conclusion and concern, at any rate, did not seem the Administration of Rodrigo Duterte. The jury is still out on whether the intelligence laws of mainland China are cause for concern for Pres. Bong Bong Marcos, and whether then inflow of mainland Chinese investments will be curtailed and limited by his Administration.

If plans push through, for instance, Huawei will provide the CCTV cameras for the planned "Safe Philippines" emergency response and monitoring system covered by a ₱20 billion contract with the China International Telecommunication Construction Corp, a mainland state owned entity.

Another mainland Chinese state-owned firm, China Telecommunications Corp., is also set to play a major role in local telecoms through its $5.4 - billion investment deal with Udenna Corporation- a company owned by Duterte's close friend Dennis Uy — to put up another telco provider for the Philippines.

There is also talk of the possibility that a Chinese firm could be bidding for, and take over, the debt-laden Hanjin Shipyard in the Subic Bay Freeport Zone. Aside with providing China with a manufacturing hub for maritime vessels, it could provide China with a center within Southeast Asia for a source of war vessels for its navy.

The stark danger, as some quarters have pointed out, is that the Chinese may gain a foothold, and eventually a listening post or even a command post, in a strategic part of the country that overlooks the South China Sea. The South China Sea of course is the very area China is coveting, and has militarized, to the detriment of the Philippines and other countries.

These are just a few examples of the insidious and dangerous effects that the implementation of China's National Law would have on the Philippines.

And if the President of the Philippines, whoever he might be, knowingly allows Chinese citizens and businesses into our country despite that law, he would be complicit in undermining the freedom and integrity of the Philippines.

And the supreme irony would be if China produces out of the Han Jin Shipyard war and coast guard vessels that would and could keep Philippine ships, specially fishing vessels, from plying Philippine seas.

(REE, 16 June 2019)

....

34
Sinagtala Ng Bayani

O mahal na Bayan ko,
Dumating na sa iyong mundo
Ang lubhang sakim ng takipsilim.
Nasaan ang tala sa langit dumilim?

Tayo ay taos pusong lalaban
Na ibalik ang liwanag sa Bayan,
Na ibalik ang Diyos natin banal
Sa Pilipinas nating minamahal.

Nasaan ang duyan ng
Mga magiting na handang
Mamatay para sa iyo, Bayan?
Ibalik ang giting sa ating kabayan!

Lalaban tayo mga anakbayan
Para sa ating sariling kasarinlan;

Ang perlas nating silanganan
Ipagtangol hanggang kamatayan.

Pilipinas aming minumutya.
Pugad ka ng luha at maralita.
Ikaw ay alab ng aming mga puso,
Aming lupain ng bulaklak at ginto.
Pilipinas tayo ay makakalaya,
Dala ang liwanag ng sinagtala
At simoy ng hanging amihan.
Pag-Asa ng ating Bayan.

Sa manlulupig di tayo pasisiil,
Haharapin natin lahat ng taksil,
Ibabalik ng bayani ang sinagtala
Sa mahal nating Inang Bansa.

(Raffy Evangelista 20 November 2021)

....

35
Gago And The Four Way Test

We have been excoriated for being "Gago" if we believe! Are we also "Gago" if we do not believe? Are we to be damned if we do, and damned if we don't?

How can the Man's word be trusted on anything? He makes so many declarartions on matters of serious concerns and later claims what he declared are merely "jokes!" How can he claim leadership of a country if everything he says is, or can be turned into a joke?

His average jokes are lewd, or grotesque, or very bad taste. How can such jokes be the mark of a true leader? How are we to react, what are we to do, when his off color jokes are so bad that they do not qualify as jokes at all despite his claims and the claims of his subalterns to the contrary?

The dictionary defines the noun "joke" as "a thing that someone says to cause amusement or laughter, specially a story with a funny punch line," and as a verb as "talking humorously or flippantly." Clearly from these definitions, lewd and grotesque jokes do not qualify as true jokes of humor. More accurately, they are non-jokes since they lack humor and are not funny.

Why then do people laugh and applaud non-jokes? Maybe the joke is on them, being syncophants all. Perhaps they are willing to do anything to please the master or the perceived person in authority.

The "joke" of this Man about sticking his fingers into the private parts of a sleeping woman fails the funny and humorous test miserably. My parents and grandparents, my school teachers and responsible authority figures would have been mortified by this so called joke. My elders always taught me not to entertain this type of jokes, including so called green jokes, because they really are demeaning insults told at the expense of others, many times women.

Now when this Man calls for religious leaders, or anyone else for that matter, to be killed, how can anyone in his right mind call that a joke? This "killer" joke goes far,far beyond green jokes, and even the "joke" about molesting a sleeping woman. This is about making light of murder plain and simple. People in their right minds do not make jokes about killing others. Which then raises the question: Is the Man in his right mind, or is he in fact telling the truth when he says he has ordered people to be killed?

Now, what would this make of his rabid followers and fence sitters who laugh at this brand of "jokes" of the Man, of sexual molestation and killing? Of killing bishops and religious leaders? I wonder if these followers would still laugh if the Man turns to them one day and says, " I will have you killed!" Can his band of merry men still manage to laugh at this joke without some trepidation that the Man may in fact mean it? Tough call! How can you still laugh when someone threatens your life? But his followers were seen laughing in national television when this Man said that religious leaders should be killed. Are these followers themselves of the "right mind?" Obviously, these followers are a band of jokers not in their right minds either. This is a case of "birds of the same feather all flocking together while sharing a dark, dicey side with the Man they adulate!

There is a more serious mind problem related to the proclivity of this Man to make jokes. If we are to follow His lead, we must know when he is serious or not. We must be able to determine what his intentions and directions are. His position of responsibility bears with it the gravitas of the highest office of the land. We have the right to know when He is joking or not. It does not help anyone, specially the Man himself, if we are called "gago" whenever we believe what he proclaims. If we can't take the Man on his word, if we have to read between the lines of everything he says, what does that say of the Man himself? That he can't be trusted to mean what he says? A practical consequence of being called "gago" often enough for believing what the Man says is that we might over time tune out and stop believing. Where does that leave the Man, the office of responsibility he holds, and the gravitas it represents? If people are left confused and discombubulated by this Man's jokes, who then will lead? Who then will follow?

The equation is simple. We need to know the truth. Leadership means precisely that: To Lead! NOT To Mislead! If the people never know whether the Man is joking or not, they are being misled away from the truth, the inevitable consequence, simply put, will be a failure of leadership. "Truth, and What and When it is the Truth" has become a main life issue for many Filipinos these days. Truth has become so opaque because of the manipulation of what is and what isn't. Is it fair to ask this Leadership, "Are you coming or going?" "Where are you taking us?" "Where are you leading us?" "Lead, for heaven's sake! Enough of jokes already!"

We can learn from Rotary International's 4 Way Test: 1) Is it the truth? 2) Is it fair to all concerned? 3) Will it build good will and better friendships? 4) Will it be beneficial to all concerned? Sadly, one can never be certain if the things this Man utters are the truth. Maybe if the Man applied this Rotary 4Way Test to the things he says and does, he would not be facing the investigation of the ICC for the thousands of EJKs that he supposedly is responsible for.

(REE, 19 July 2023)

....

36
Haikus On Life

Go
*My father led me
To the forest edge,
And said, "Go your way!"*

Where Do I go?
"But there are no tracks,"
I said. "Where am I to go?"
As he bade me goodbye.

Farewell
The mist covered him
As he disappeared in the
Setting of the sun.

Life's Beginning
My own life began when
I trudged down forest trails
As stars led my way.

Discovery of Self
I found myself when
My father let me go on
Into the unknown.

Flying
His was the wisdom
Of the ages that allowed
Me to fly to the skies.

(Raf Evangelista, 23 February 2023)

....

37
Haiku Outside The Box

Outside The Box
Think and act outside

The box to achieve your goals,
Beyond four corners.

Fly Higher
Fly the kite higher,
Reach up to touch the morning,
And dream of flying.

Melting Moon
The moon melts into
The brooding sky as the sun
Rises to awake.

Sinews
Sinews of the hearts
Wrestle between mine and yours.
Could we be in love?

White Crosses
In rigid, straight lines,
In military cadence,
White crosses marching.

Stolen
Where have hugs gone,
The embraces and kisses?
The virus stole them.

Inner Eye
The flimsy dress draped
Across your taut, tense bodice
Scans my inner eye.

Choices
Choices reflect all
The life values that lead us...
What to love ... and hate.

God's Touch
I look at my hands

And wonder how many times
God touched them with love.

Mind Painting
Faded photographs,
Old with age, but repainted
Freshly by the mind.

Recall
Why do we recall –
The flower in bloom, failing?
The sun slowly rising?

What Once Was
See through the absence.
Be grateful for what once was –
The lives and loves shared!

Conquering Love
But love conquers death.
Love once freely given grows,
And will never end.

Plant
Turn the soil over.
Planting is a gift of time.
Watch the flowers bloom.

Be Still
Silence harried thoughts.
Be still to gestures of love,
Which will calm the soul!

Persuasion
Like the sun rising,
Love sways the uncommitted,
Without coercion.

On My Way
I'll be on my way,

*Even as my heart's breaking
And my tears are gone.*

Spring Is Coming
*The wind sings it's song.
Is it sad? It is cold, but
Spring is almost here.*

Small Things
*Count Do small things with love,
If big things are difficult.
Big, small, count the same.*

True Love
*Love is not feeling.
Love is what you do with it ...
Giving and forgiving.*

Happy Lines
*The happiest lines
I can offer are the lines
Painted by rainbows!*

Beyond Borders
*Care beyond borders,
And roaring seas:
Share!*

Remember Fondly
*Think of me fondly
When the stars cover heaven,
But also deep darkness.*

Come With The Sun
*You may disappear
 When you feel you are not you.
Just come with the sun.*

Beginning End
The end beginning,

The constant waves buffet me.
I feel like drowning.

Bird Sketch
Birds, perched on a tree,
Outline night's face that welcomes
The gold of sunset.

Heaven's Kiss
The moon reaches down
To kiss the rolling waves with
The touch of heaven.

Colors of the Sun
A thousand colors
As the sun rises eastward.
What then at sunset?

Why?
Why must darkness come?
The sun shines during the day.
The moon at night time.

Where Beauty Lies
Don't check my face for Looks.
Rather look to my heart
If beauty lies there.

God's Brush
Speak to a thousand
Rainbows across the heavens
Painted by God's brush.

Blindness Is Deadly
Cross the street of life
With both eyes fully open.
Blindness is deadly.

Swim
Let me walk with you

As you wade through deep waters.
I know how to swim.

Reaping Love
I came with nothing
But love ... the love that I am
Now going home with.

One Last Time
He closed his eyes in
One final moment of time,
His hand clasped in hers.

Sleep
Don't call the doctor.
I just want to go to sleep
With your hand in mine.

Understand
When harsh winds lash o'er
The loveless land, the sky
Whispers, "Understand!"

Racism
Like a bad winter,
Dawn has finally broken...
And all colors clash.

Humanizing White
The white man who killed
Asian women recently,
Was sex humanized!

I Matter
Cross the great divide.
Leave all that does not matter,
But do not leave me.

Dawn And Sunset
Enveloped by dawn,

Am still enthralled by light streams
Of the setting sun.

What Do You See?
Do you see shadows
Dancing in the light of day
Or only daylight?

Dance Of Rain Drops
Tiny droplets dance
On this side of the rainbow
Straddling the mountains.

Will You Remember?
Now that you are gone,
Will you remember sometimes
I once held your hand.

Flying
Flying by the seat of My pants,
I'll figure it out
As I breeze along.

Lead Me
Where does the road lead,
Up or down, straight or circles?
Hold my hand. Lead me.

All Colored
Why do whites kill blacks?
Why do blacks go after browns?
All are of color!

No Wrinkles
Love has no wrinkles
Provided the heart is true.
Stay with me, my love.

At the Rainbow's End
You can chase your dream

If you don't stop at rainbows.
Gold is at the end!

Through It All
Through the good and bad,
Through the darkness and sunshine,
I will be with you.

Fingers
Fingers of the wind
Softly stroke the tall grass and
Strum a lullaby.

....

38
Populism And Inaction, At What Cost?

Rodrigo Roa Duterte as a leader has been a vessel for all the worst elements of the Filipino nation. And he is a cheap, soulless bully besides, which is the very essence of the populist strong man he portends to be. We've never had such a crass excuse for a President as Rodrigo Roa Duterte. We've never had a populist at the helm of leadership so completely deserving of scorn and yet so small in the office that it almost seems a waste of time and energy to summon up the requisite contempt. But this populism has, and will have a price. We must act, if we are to avoid having to pay that price.

To simply say nothing and do nothing about his brand of populism could mean planting the seeds for the death of our Republic. It could die, if not now then later on, when the pernicious effects of his reign are fully in place. It could die in the empty hands of an empty man who feels nothing but his own imaginary greatness, and who cannot find in himself the decency simply to shut up even when it is in his best interest to do so. But it could also die because we allowed and encouraged him to do what he seems to do best, bullying, without restraint.

Presidents don't have to be heroes to be good presidents. They just have to realize that their humanity is our common humanity, and that their political commonwealth is our political commonwealth too. This cannot be achieved by a populist president whose only concept of leadership and favorite past time are contempt and the bullying of others, specially the weak.

Bullying by its very nature is divisive. National bullying is a political vision that is determined to to turn Filipino against Filipino, in order to intimidate and maintain control. It is a political vision that is beyond reckless, and is, quite simply, a prescription for political extinction. Division is not the answer. If we want the Filipino People to have a viable alternative in the future, the name of the game is addition rather than subtraction, multiplication rather than division.

Above all this, there is an inherent contradiction between being a public official/public servant in the service of the people, and a public bully. A public bully simply refuses to acknowledge this fundamental democratic precept - the people are the boss because "Sovereignty resides in the people and all governmental authority emanates from them.

Classical paychology teaches that there are three types of bullying- Verbal Bullying - the saying or writing of mean things.

Verbal bullying includes teasing; name calling; inappropriate sexual or racial comments; taunting; and threatening to cause harm.

Social Bullying - sometimes to as relational bullying. It involves hurting someone's reputation or relationships. Social bullying includes leaving someone out a group on purpose; telling children not to befriend others; spreading rumors about someone; embarassing someone in public.

Physical Bullying - involves hurting a person's body or possessions. Physical bullying includes: hitting; kicking; pinching; physically molesting; spitting;tripping, pushing; taking or breaking someone's things; making mean or rude gestures.

Clearly, Duterte has been guilty of verbal bullying - he is given to name calling; he has uttered inappropriate sexual comments; he loves to taunt others; and often threatens others with physical harm.

He often engages in social bullying - he says ugly things about others; he loves to embarrass his critics in public.

He is given to physical bullying, at least in so far as rude hand gestures go. He also loves to brag/joke how he has killed before or how he has sexually molested women.

We have adapted far too easily to a crude and coarse dialoque emanating from this leader that we would never have tolerated from foreigners. We have become numb to language that is unbecoming of public servants at any level of government. And thus we do nothing. Or on the other extreme, we applaud!

Such theatrics may excite a particular base for while. Who can forget how the German people adulated that notorious populist leader, Adolph Hitler? But most of us would like to believe that eventually common sense and the ingrained decency of the Filipino will prevail. And if and when that happens, the President's base could, sooner or later, become smaller with every new slight, with every new insult, and eventually the source be castrated.

That is precisely what happened in Germany. That is what happened in Pol Pot's Cambodia. That is what happened in EDSA 1986.

We must say "no" to bullying. We must say "no" to populism.

Until then, our suppliant inaction to national populist bullying is costing us big time, at the risk of our democracy's political extinction!

(REE, 8 January 2019)

....

39
Haiku Selection

Friends
Hand in hand through years,
Sun soaked in the warmth of years,
Amidst wrinkled smiles.
(REE, 19 March 2019)

Cleansing Rain
The old horse plods in
The swirling mud, then canters
To the cleansing rain.
(REE, 20 March 2019)

Letting Go
I can let go of
Power and wealth, but not of
The love now distant.
(REE, 22 April 2019)

The Road
Don't pass up today,
Tomorrow may never come,
The road winds on.
(REE, 28 June 2019)

Heaven's Fire
Fire from the heavens,
Deep rumblings before the storm,

The anvil of God.
(REE, 30 November 2019)

Soar
I do not pander
To those who would push and shove.
Soaring, should I care?
(REE, 11 December 2019)

Kiss
Kiss the rains falling
Over scorched, burning mountains.
Trees, what remain, weep.
(REE, 25 December 2019)

Trash
Trash in parks and roads,
Trash amongst our leadership,
Trash in minds and hearts.
(REE, 27 December 2019)

Burning
The earth is burning.
Is it God's wrath or our own
Stupidity? Both?
(REE, 5 January 2020)

Home
Going home is just
Beyond the bridge of darkness
To light all over.
(REE, 7 January 2020)

Indifferent
I, indifferent?
Should I care, if you do not
Make a difference?
(REE, 8 January 2020)

War Rumblings

Flashes in the dark.
Drums of war rumble, but rains
Drench the roaring fires.
(REE, 11 January 2020)

Scorched
The tear slowly falls,
The last of many that fell.
The scorched heart rages.
(REE, 12 January 2020)

White Fire
Once the line is crossed
Where white fire both burns and soothes,
There is no return.
(REE, 29 January 2020)

Love of Self
Why must it be so?
There's a lot of self in you,
Taking, not giving.
(REE, 3 February 2020)

Love's Meaning
Building means giving,
But love simply comes to naught
Without forgiving.
(REE, 4 February 2020)

Unseen Piper
We all march to the
Tune of the unseen piper's
Haunting melody.
(REE, 5 February 2020)

Ate
I reach out my hand
To one I loved all these years,
Borne from the same womb.
(REE, 5 February 2020)

Go low, Why?
Why must we go low?
We can't go high anymore,
Because others won't?
(REE, 7 February 2020)

We Are More
They win by making
You feel that you are alone ...
There are more of us.
(REE, 9 February 2020)

My World
There is joy that's found
In simplicity of life,
The world I hope for.
(REE, 15 February 2020)

Populism
Not allowed to speak,
Not allowed to criticize,
The freedom bell tolls.
(REE, 29 February 2020)

Once, Valentine
A kaleidoscope
Of many moments now gone,
A portrait of love.
(REE, 14 March 2020)

Political Winds
Shifting of the winds,
Where will they carry me to,
Peace or turbulence?
(REE, 22 March 2020)

Not There
In the darkness,
I Raised my hand to stroke your brow,

But you were not there.
(REE, 27 March 2020)

Taho
The vendor searches
Forlornly for the children
Who used buy taho.
(REE, 30 March 2020)

Hungry
Hunger stalks the land
From dark sea to fearful sea,
Waves from same waters.
(REE, 1 April 2020)

On My Own
I bow my head as
I hear the clap of thunder.
I am on my own.
(REE, 10 April 2020)

Broken Fingers
I held out my hand.
You refused to walk with me...
Broken fingers
(REE, 21 April 2020)

Fly With Me
Why do you have doubts?
Before the sun disappears,
Fly away with me.
(REE, 29 April 2020)

Silence
The laughter shattered,
A tear ripples on the pond,
Then awkward silence.
(REE, 12 May 2020)

Goodbyes

Why are there goodbyes?
Do things really have to end?
Go then. Say nothing.
(REE, 25 May 2020)

Life and Death
Defeat death in life.
Do not be pushed by darkness,
Till death takes you home.
(REE, 1 June 2020)

Remember
I am heartbroken.
Your soul may not remember
Me when I am gone.

Junkyard
The junkyard filled with
Bones of the old forgotten,
Rusting in the wind.

Heartbeats
Nothing, nothing stirs,
But for faint, gentle throbbings,
Beating of a heart.

Sunrise
Sunrise once again
Beyond dark skies and thunder,
The clear horizon.

Like Yesterday
Standing on the porch
Watching you walk away,it
Seems like yesterday.

Morning Will Come
The morning will come
From where I shall keep searching.
For now the night grows.

Mask

The mask clouds my breathe,
So that I can hardly breath
The air that we breath!

Road

On the lonely road,
Too far to travel back,
Blackness up ahead.

Thunder

The rolling heavens
Stirs up golden clouds
With claps of thunder.

So Far

You're so far away…
Can you even hear my voice?
You stopped listening.

Shadows

Shadows race across
The grasslands, chasing after
Clouds that paint the sky.

Promise

I embrace tonight
To be able to promise
Light for tomorrow.

Seeing

It is in the dark
That I can see the sunshine;
I close my eyes now.

Evers

Why are there endings?
Are evers not forevers?
Each second ticked, lost?

Never
I was crestfallen.
I'd never see you again
Smiling through the rain.

Broken Pieces
Broken pieces of
Today dumped in the dust bins
Of forgotten days.

Storm
It is storming outside,
But I do not really care.
I have shut the door.

We Cannot Breathe
Your knee's on our necks,
Ours, not just George Floyd's,
And we cannot breathe.
(REE, 31 May 2020)

I Can't Breathe
Mama, I can't breathe!
The morning is turning dark.
Now I cannot see.
(REE, 1 June 2020)

Drained
I am drained of smiles...
Lost behind the drapes, the sun!
Please bless me with tears.
(REE, 4 June 2020)

Once More
Before the day ends,
Let me embrace you once more,
Before darkness comes.

Take A Knee

We are connected,
All our minds, hearts and souls are.
Let us take a knee.

With You
I will walk with you
No matter the churning skies.
Your hand guides the way.

Everyone
Everybody smiles,
Everybody cries, sometimes,
Even through the sun.

Dont Turn Away
Don't just turn away,
I have been waiting so long.
I ask you to stay.

Void
There's a void in me.
It's been fifteen years ago.
It's time to let go.

Rainbows on the Desert Floor
Carpets of flowers
On the arid desert floor,
Rainbows without rain!

(REE, 27 August 2020)

....

40

"Minced oaths"

I can't recall if I wrote this piece or is someone else did. I therefore treat it as a repost. I share it because I grew up with the hilarious language of my times, from childhood to adulthood.

When I was young, folks used words like "durn," "doggone," and "dadblame" as adjectives. "Shoot!" and "Durnit!" were common ways to express frustration. When my granny got particularly upset, she would say "Fiddlesticks!"

Words such as these are called "minced oaths." They are socially permissible substitutes for similar words that are considered vulgar or profane.

Until the late 19th century, most English language expletives ("cuss words," as I learned to call them) were profanities—irreverent uses of words taken from religion or the Bible, words such as "God," "hell," or "damnation," for example. Of course, it was coarse and socially unacceptable to use such words irreverently (profanely), so minced oaths such as "gosh," "heck," and "tarnation," arose as substitutes. One of the most common early minced oaths was "Zounds!," used to express surprise and a substitute for the profane "God's wounds!"

By 1900, as blasphemy became less shocking, obscenities and vulgarity began to replace profanity as the expletives of choice, with the most commonly used expletives/swear words being derived from words for body parts, bodily wastes, and sex. Naturally as these expletives became more common, so did minced oath substitutes like "shoot," "shucks," "flip," and "fudge."

An observer of language in the 21st century might reasonably wonder whether we are witnessing the end of minced oaths. Nowadays, more than at any time in prior history, there seems to be little aversion or adverse consequence to the use of expletives that not long ago would have been considered outrageous and offensive vulgarities. With the normalizing of such words, the need for minced oath substitutes diminishes. So perhaps

minced oaths are becoming a thing of the past. If so, I'm going to miss them, doggone-it.
CTTO

(REE, 22 July 2023)

....

41
Homily Of Archbishop Socrates Villegas - worth thinking about and passing on –

Lingayen-Dagupan Archbishop Socrates Villegas wrote the following reflection for the 16th Sunday in Ordinary Time, July 23, on the viral video of Pura Luka Vega, a Filipino drag queen who dressed up as Jesus. Rappler is publishing this piece with Villegas' permission.

My dear brothers and sisters in the Church of Lingayen-Dagupan:

Wheat and weeds sprouted together putting the wheat at risk (Mt 13: 24-30). Before they sprang and grew together in the same field, both wheat and weeds were first small seeds. The seeds were sown by the farmer. The seeds of the weeds were sown by the enemy. But remember: Both good and evil started small. Both good and evil were sown unto the same field. Although they came from different hands, they grew from the same soil. Weeds harm wheat. Wheat stems do not harm weeds.

A few weeks ago, mainstream and social media carried the video of a mockery of the Ama Namin as it was sung in a drag contest of a group that call themselves a queer community. Protests were expressed. The viral video was slammed as blasphemous and grossly disrespectful.

To a certain extent, the video was a shocking scandal but it was bound to reach this untested limit in time. This video was a plunge into a deeper cliff of vulgar blasphemy. It was bound to happen in time. When did we see it coming?

The seeds for this scandalous video were already planted in the field when we allowed vulgarity by high leaders in government to become a joking matter. Our cooperative indifference and supportive laughter, as we heard those vulgarities, make us accomplices in blasphemy. This was a small beginning like the seed of weeds.

The small seeds were already planted when we chose cowardly silence as God was cursed by the highest government official. We giggled and later on voted for more officials who support such vulgarity. We were in cahoots. The seeds were planted then.

The seeds of this blasphemy were already sown by the enemies of God when the Church and our bishops were threatened with murder and called obscene and irreverent names and we quietly conspired. Loud vulgar mouths wanted Gospel teaching lips to be mute. We preferred vulgar lips to teach us instead. We conspired by our silence. We planted bad seeds.

A drag song and dance against the Ama Namin offends indeed but some matters are more offensive than this.

We call God our Father but do not treat one another as brothers and sisters? We call God our Father but nodded with approval when drug addicts were killed? Killing others made our lives safer? Is that the way to worship God as Father? They are seeds of the weeds.

Our lips pray "Hallowed be your name" and yet our hands on our gadgets confect calumny and gossip and slander? Is God's name adored by our fake news?

We have even baptized gossipers and rumormongers as Marites. These are seeds of the weeds.

We beg Him "to give us our daily bread" but accept money to sell our votes? Is God honored when we tolerate and benefit from the stolen money of public servants? Is not our acceptance of the culture of graft and plunder of public money a greater blasphemy of the Ama Namin? These are seeds of the weeds.

We ask God "to forgive us" and yet we have chosen to solve our social problems by the "extrajudicial" way (outside the court of law) by killing and later covering up for the murderers of those who were never proven guilty? How can the defenders of mass murderers and crimes against humanity pray to ask God for forgiveness when their lifestyle is its exact opposite?

In the end, we ask, "In what ways have I contributed to the vulgarity and blasphemy, desecration and profanity of language and lewdness of action against the Ama Namin?"

If we are honest and humble enough, we should be ready to admit that we planted the seeds of weeds in the past by our indifference, cowardice, and connivance. The weeds came from me. The enemy is me. I must now change MYSELF first. What great changes each of us must make!

ctto

....

42
You Are My Anchor, Lord

I may be torn and battered,

But my mast will hold.
All it needs is a little heart
That needs to be bold.

I shall not shirk from the task
That You have assigned to me.
No matter how my ship lists,
I will still come home from sea.
Stay with me, Lord, My God,
When I falter, bear me up.
So no matter how difficult
Or painful, don't let me stop.

The times that the waves
Grow unruly and restless,
And strike against the sky,
Do not leave me helpless.

I will batten down the hatches
And ask You to be my Guide
As I tread the foaming sea.
Be there always at my side.

My anchor will hold firm.
Please steady my ship at sea.
You are my Anchor, my Lord.
Without You where would I be?

You are my Anchor, Lord
If You stay here at my side.
Please hush the tossing waves
And stem the roaring tides.

need You, Lord!

(REE, 22 July 2023)

....

43
Thoughts Of One Weary, Wary And Worn Doctor

I just received this heart and gut wrenching message from one of our medical warriors fighting this pandemic war for us in the frontlines. My question to all of you: "What shall we do, what can we do to address the plight of our frontliners in white!

Too heart rending not to share.- Thoughts Of One Weary, Wary And Worn Doctor......

"Three weeks ago, my wife showed me an on-line article saying that by the end of this COVID-19 pandemic, medical doctors will be tired of their profession and will seek more satisfying (probably more lucrative, too) jobs.

At that time, I shrugged it off as nonsense, as most doctors (including yours truly) go into this profession as a calling and with tons of passion for it. Personally, I've never seen myself as anything but, so in essence, this is what I grew up wanting to be, and this is what I ended up becoming.

"It's just one big hullabaloo. This pandemic will be over in time, and us doctors will be better appreciated after."

Yeah, right.

Five months after this pandemic started in Wuhan and a little over two months since Enhanced Community Quarantine (now that's a mouthful) was declared, we are, by no means at all, much closer to finding a solution to it all.

But that's okay.

For those in the know, or for those who actually give a fuck, the whole "Stay-at-home" order and this quarantine shiznit was never meant to be a solution to the problem. It was meant to buy health officials enough time to come up with something, with the least number of infections possible, and consequently, fewest number of deaths.

Ideally.

So yeah, while we haven't exactly flattened the curve, the good news is that... well, there is no good news.

Our economy is, pardon the language, in a shithole. But who cares. It was headed there anyway, with our incompetent leaders (I'm being polite, by the way). It was destined for that, with China waiting in the wings to be our "savior."

Our health care system is on life-support. But who cares. Doctors, after all, were useless. Remember? "Salita nang salita wala namang ginagawa, complain nang complain."

Our government is leaving us out on our own. But who cares. They get VIP testing, mananitas, "human compassion" and other entitlements. All while we barely get through the days at home or at work.

Frankly, that's the exhausting part.

Never mind this virus cloud hanging over our collective heads. Never mind the lack of PPEs for health care workers. Never mind the alarming rates of infection and deaths of nurses, doctors, allied medical professionals. Never mind the endless stream of patients painstakingly waiting for their test results to come out.

It's fine.

We can handle these things.

It's the ineptitude, the callousness, the stupidity, the insensitivity, the sense of entitlement of our government and health care leaders that's burning us out. Burning everyone out. The doctors, nurses, bank employees, supermarket staff, drivers, delivery guys, etc. All the little guys.

I am proud to be a doctor. Always have been, always will be.

I am proud to work alongside nurses, pharmacists, nursing aides, utility workers, and other hospital staff. These people work day-in, day-out, night-in, night-out, not just to collect another paycheck. It's because this is what we swore to do- serve and care for patients, regardless of color, creed, affiliation.

The thing is... I'm beginning to distance myself from the very profession I swore to.

Yesterday, I declined to take an emergency case at one of the hospitals I'm affiliated with, despite it not conflicting with anything on my schedule.

It's the first time I have ever done that. For the first time in 6 plus years of being an anesthesiologist, I was not excited to do what I do best.

And it was because I have grown weary, wary and worn.

Weary from the shit that we've been subjected to by the very people we pay to serve us (such high taxes, all for naught!).

Wary from this virus that has killed some close friends and colleagues, and a constant threat to the well-being of my family.

Worn from just being a doctor, a healthcare worker.

I'd never thought the day would come when I would have second thoughts about being one.

Those who know me well know that the operating room is my happy place. It's called work, but I like to call it art. The OR is where I'm comfortable, and it's where I work my magic and do what I am good at.

I pride myself in coming to my ORs prepared, punctual and passionate about what I do. I come locked-in and ready to go.

I always tell my residents, Be excited about coming to the OR. Learn from every patient, every case you do. Treat each procedure as a learning experience.

Because that's what I live by: being excited about going to work, because it's an opportunity to better myself at my craft, a chance to learn and become more.

But for a confluence of reasons, yesterday, I wasn't up to it.

I never thought I'd see the day when I was unmotivated to go to work. Maybe it was fear, maybe it was fatigue, maybe it was just "fuck it, you know?"

At the start of this rant (that's all I'm good at these days, it seems), I mentioned about my wife telling me about that article saying that doctors will want to get out of this profession when the COVID19 dust settles. Sure, I brushed it off then, but you know what? Maybe the article was right. Maybe.

Do I still want to be a doctor when all of this ends? It's the only thing I know how to be, and yet, the very nature of me having second thoughts about it is… disturbing to me.

Like I said. Worn out. Weary. Wary. In whatever order you want.

It's not the virus that's going to kill us. It's the stupidity of people tasked with leading us.

Fuck. …

………

If you're still reading this, then man, I think you'll agree with me that it has gotten pretty depressing real quick.

I'm speaking as a physician, but I'm sure other professions out there are feeling the exact same thing about their work. Nothing too big, nothing too small.

Weary. Wary. Worn.

I'm trying to think of some happy anecdote or some insightful idea right now that can flip this narrative into something upbeat and inspiring, but nothing's coming to me. It's hopeless.

Then again, I guess that's the sad reality of the state of our lives here in this country. Hopelessness.

So to everyone out there who's working and trying to fend for themselves in this time of crisis, my hat's off to you.

Hang in there. Survive.

Like my wife says, at least we're alive. ☺"

My reaction:

This is so true, depressing, but true. Even in an armed conflict, soldiers are willing to lay down their life. But an enlightened, imaginative and compassionate leadership is the most basic ingredient for the soldiers to keep fighting. Having served for the cause of our army veterans for over 15 years, that is a principle that I came to understand and embrace. War is not the time to have clueless, bambling, rudderless and thoughtless leadership. It seems that is what we have now. But God bless all you Medical warriors for doing your utmost during these trying times.

CTTO

....

44
Happy Birthday EDSA!

You are 35 years old today. Many are saying you are a disappointment. You were supposed to be our "miracle" baby, and we had so many expectations. You were born a product of many fathers and mothers, each with an idealisation of you. On hindsight, giving birth to you was the easy part. Nurturing and seeing you grow wasn't.

But I don't agree with some that you shouldn't have been born at all, that you were a mistake. Parenting democracy is a tough job and it never stops. I cannot imagine life without you. I cannot agree that we would have been better off had we continued to be a country plundered and ruled with impunity, or a toxic home of cronies, human rights violators, militarisation, stifling of dissent, propagandists peddling lies and a coterie of yes men.

I'm happy to have been there at your birth. The miracle should have been about us parenting you better. Well, here we are now. Thank God for the next generation. Maybe they'll understand you better and see the potential of democracy as infinitely better than throwing you back to toxic authoritarianism.

It isn't going to be easy and I'll still be nostalgic for the scent of fresh grass trampled by the churning gears of heavy tanks,the scent of tear gas and flowers,the sight of tears from fear and joy.

Happy Birthday EDSA!

CTTO

....